Fruitful

Aligning Your Goals
with His Plan

You are worth it!
AC

Constance Shelby

bookVillages

Fruitful: Aligning Your Goals with His Plan
© 2024 Constance Shelby

All rights reserved. No part of this publication may be reproduced in any form without written permission from Book Villages, P.O. Box 64526, Colorado Springs, CO 80962. www.bookvillages.com

ISBN: 978-1-95756-629-0

Cover and Interior Design by Niddy Griddy Design, Inc.

Unless otherwise identified, all Scripture quotations in this publication are taken from The Holy Bible, English Standard Version. ESV® Text Edition: 2016. Copyright © 2001 by Crossway Bibles, a publishing ministry of Good News Publishers. Holy Bible, New International Version®, NIV® Copyright ©1973, 1978, 1984, 2011 by Biblica, Inc.® Used by permission. All rights reserved worldwide. Scripture taken from the New King James Version®. NKJV Copyright © 1982 by Thomas Nelson. Used by permission. All rights reserved. New American Standard Bible®, NASB1995 Copyright © 1960, 1971, 1977, 1995 by The Lockman Foundation. All rights reserved.

Printed in the United States of America
1 2 3 4 5 6 7 8 Printing / Year 28 27 26 25 24

I am the true vine, and my Father is the vinedresser. Every branch in me that does not bear fruit he takes away, and every branch that does bear fruit he prunes, that it may bear more fruit. Already you are clean because of the word that I have spoken to you. Abide in me, and I in you. As the branch cannot bear fruit by itself, unless it abides in the vine, neither can you, unless you abide in me. I am the vine; you are the branches. Whoever abides in me and I in him, he it is that bears much fruit, for apart from me you can do nothing.

You did not choose me, but I chose you and appointed you that you should go and bear fruit and that your fruit should abide, so that whatever you ask the Father in my name, he may give it to you.

John 15:1-5, 16

To my girls, I pray you always remember to slow enough to hear that "still small voice."

Sweet sister,
We cannot bear fruit by ourselves.
May we always pursue the vine.

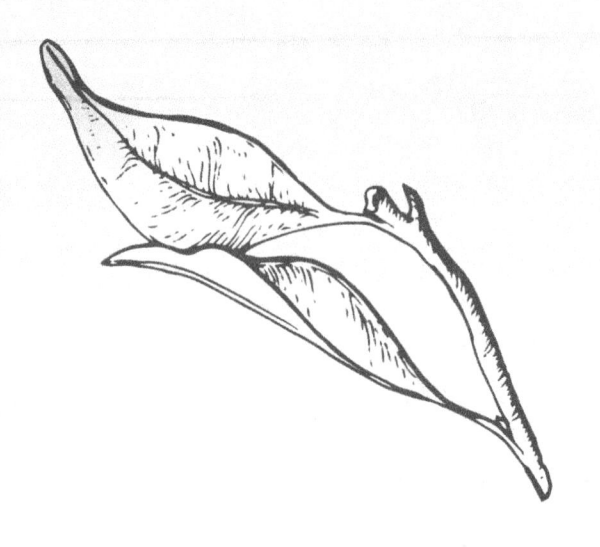

Fruitful
ALIGNING YOUR GOALS WITH HIS PLANS

INTRODUCTION

All too often we separate our earthly desires from our prayer life. I don't believe it is always purposeful, but as women of an instantaneous and busy world, we tend to take matters of improvement into our own hands before asking God if this is the direction He wants us to go. Reflecting back on progress made throughout my life, I can confidently say that the sweetest fruit grew during the times that I relied on God and not on my own stewing and stressing. Oftentimes, this growth came in a season when my circumstances were too big a burden for me to bear alone so I had to lean in to Him. The funny thing is, time and time again, I have pushed myself to the point of becoming overwhelmed and facing disaster before finally succumbing to His will. Over time and with lots of reflection, I am learning this way is harder and much more exhausting. And definitely not the way God would prefer.

God does not need our help, only our obedience. And in this crazy world of "always on," I believe women are finding themselves more overwhelmed with all their to-dos and in less conversation with God. Without that direct line of communication, we are simply spinning on a hamster wheel wishing and waiting for most of our days.

Along with that, we are so consumed in our wants and have such little time to be still that many of us are walking down roads that He doesn't want us on, or at least taking paths that are longer and more treacherous than He intended. Sis, we are making it harder on ourselves because we refuse to let the guard down—sit still and lean in.

SETTING GOALS

I believe in goal setting.

Planning and preparing for a positive change and working to achieve it can build our character and make us a better steward of God's creation and of others. In one of His parables in Luke 14, Jesus speaks of having a goal and considering the plan to reach it. Proverbs mentions planning and working hard several times. It is no secret to believers that we are here on this earth to do God's works, and those works require us to have some sense of direction. Otherwise, we will be all over the map, trying different things daily, never bearing any fruit!

However, over my time of working with thousands of women to lose weight, I have noticed that so many of us are missing the mark with our goal setting.

Oftentimes we set goals from our flesh that sound picture-perfect and reflect the world's ideas of what hustle and success look like . . . never seeking God in the making.

Do not conform to the pattern of this world, but be transformed by the renewing of your mind. Then you will be able to test and approve what God's will is—his good, pleasing and perfect will. (Romans 12:2, NIV)

Other times we have a pretty decent goal set, maybe even one that came from God, yet we don't do the consistent work needed to actually achieve it.

And let us not grow weary of doing good, for in due season we will reap, if we do not give up. (Galatians 6:9)

Even more, we tend to turn our goal into something so complicated and distant that our motivation starts to peter out and it becomes easier to look the other way.

Whether we realize it or not, this cycle causes a deep-rooted feeling of failure within our souls that can begin to present itself as a label stamped on our brains and in our hearts. We convince ourselves that we will never change anyway . . . so, what's the use?

It's too hard.
It takes too much time.
I am not strong enough.
I don't have the willpower.
I can't do this.

God did not intend for us to be this way. Read the following verses to learn what God wants for us.

But as for you, be strong and do not give up, for your work will be rewarded. (2 Chronicles 15:7, NIV)

The plans of the diligent lead to profit as surely as haste leads to poverty. (Proverbs 21:5, NIV)

Whatever you do, work at it with all your heart, as working for the Lord, not for human masters, since you know that you will receive an inheritance from the Lord as a reward. It is the Lord Christ you are serving. (Colossians 3:23-24, NIV)

And I am sure of this, that he who began a good work in you will bring it to completion at the day of Jesus Christ. (Philippians 1:6)

Our goals should reflect His path for us, no matter how small we may think they are. And even if we feel hopeless on some days, if we feel right with God about the goal, we can rest in knowing that He will give us the perseverance to continue. After all, it's His strength we should be relying on anyway, right? As you read these verses, you will be encouraged knowing that God is with you.

For no word from God will ever fail. (Luke 1:37, NIV)

Unless the Lord builds the house, the builders labor in vain. Unless the Lord watches over the city, the guards stand watch in vain. (Psalm 127:1, NIV)

In their hearts humans plan their course, but the Lord establishes their steps. (Proverbs 16:9, NIV)

Do not work for food that spoils, but for food that endures to eternal life, which the Son of Man will give you. For on him God the Father has placed his seal of approval.
(John 6:27, NIV)

What good is it, my brothers and sisters, if someone claims to have faith but has no deeds? Can such faith save them? Suppose a brother or a sister is without clothes and daily food. If one of you says to them, "Go in peace; keep warm and well fed," but does nothing about their physical needs, what good is it? In the same way, faith by itself, if it is not accompanied by action, is dead.

But someone will say, "You have faith; I have deeds."

Show me your faith without deeds, and I will show you my faith by my deeds. You believe that there is one God. Good! Even the demons believe that—and shudder.

You foolish person, do you want evidence that faith without deeds is useless? Was not our father Abraham considered righteous for what he did when he offered his son Isaac on the altar? You see that his faith and his actions were working together, and his faith was made complete by what he did. And the scripture was fulfilled that says, "Abraham believed God, and it was credited to him as righteousness," and he was called God's friend. You see that a person is considered righteous by what they do and not by faith alone.
In the same way, was not even Rahab the prostitute considered righteous for what she did when she gave lodging to the spies and sent them off in a different direction? As the body without the spirit is dead, so faith without deeds is dead.

James 2:14-26, NIV

GOD DOESN'T JUST WANT OUR FAITH— HE WANTS OUR ACTION

Setting the goal is not enough.

We tend to want to stop there, expecting all our dreams to come true since we finally acknowledge what we want to achieve and feel God on our side in it. But the reality is, that is just the beginning. If the goal is aligned with God's desires for us, His word says we must still put the steps into action to get there. God will not magically provide weight loss or any other achievement without us consistently putting in the work, showing up daily and relying on his strength with each stride forward. Take time to read and meditate on these verses as you put your steps into action.

Those who work their land will have abundant food, but those who chase fantasies have no sense.
(Proverbs 12:11, NIV)

For even when we were with you, we gave you this rule: "The one who is unwilling to work shall not eat." We hear that some among you are idle and disruptive. They are not busy; they are busybodies. Such people we command and urge in the Lord Jesus Christ to settle down and earn the food they eat.
(2 Thessalonians 3:10-12, NIV)

The hand of the diligent will rule, But the lazy man will be put to forced labor. (Proverbs 12:24, NKJV)

When you shall eat of the fruit of your hands, You will be happy and it will be well with you.
(Psalm 128:2, NASB 1995)

All hard work brings a profit, but mere talk leads only to poverty. (Proverbs 14:23, NIV)

You get the picture. God wants us to lean on Him to reveal to us our goals and also consistently come to Him for help achieving them. And then turn around and praise Him for His faithfulness! If we are willing to lean on Him and do our part, I believe God will gradually let us in on His plans for us and guide us best on how to get there.

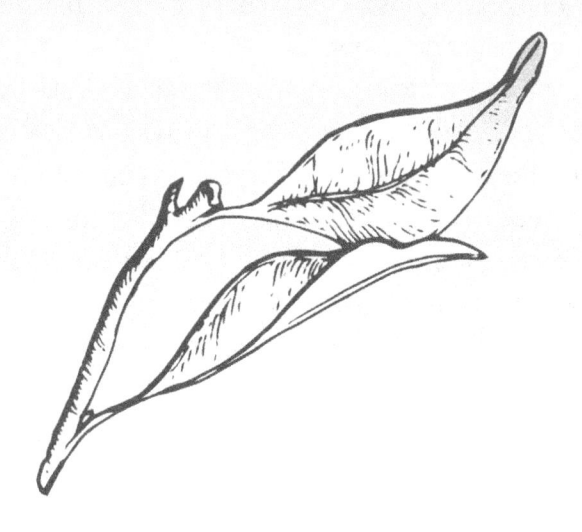

MAKING A CAKE

When encouraging my weight loss clients, I often talk about making a cake when striving to reach their goals.

Waaaaaait! What, Constance? Weight loss and making a cake?

YES! Let me explain.

I don't know about you, but when given the choice between a sheet cake and a layered cake, I am going to choose a layered cake every time. Now, there is nothing wrong with a sheet cake—one layer of cake with one layer of icing.

But . . .

There is something so much better about a layer cake—all the cake and icing intertwined and working together to support the structure at its desired height. Each layer supporting the next to make it something strong and sturdy on the inside while looking polished and confident on the outside. It is richer no doubt.

If I am going to eat some cake, that's the kind of cake I want.

However, you know that part of what makes that layer cake so much better is the extra time and effort that was put into creating it.

The baker had to bake several pans of cake and spend extra time and care on each layer to ensure that the next layer would go on just as sturdy as the last. Laying one cake down, letting it cool, putting icing on it, and getting it near perfect, then adding that next layer.

Slowly . . .

Intentionally . . .

Realistically . . .

If the baker had thrown all the warm cake layers on at once and then smeared icing all over, everything would slide off into a huge mess.

It would be a wasted cake.

One that went into the trash to never be thought of again.

While it sounds silly for a baker to do this in the kitchen, it is often exactly how we approach our goals. We decide we want to accomplish something and then hunt out and attempt every single thing we *could* do to help us reach our goal. Never taking into account the fact that maybe we aren't quite ready for all that warm cake and icing to go on at once!

So, as we head into the next sections, I encourage you to be like the expert baker and take your time and be intentional with each and every layer. Start with one thing (the bottom cake layer) and spend a lot of time there. Make that effort towards your goal something that becomes consistent, and, like a habit, polishing it well (the bottom icing layer) before you move on to the next step (the next cake layer). This is how goals are reached and forever changes are made—consistently and intentionally.

If you approach your goal this way, before you know it, you will be putting the finishing touches on your cake with so much pride, but more than that, with confidence that the foundation is sturdy and strong and will not crumble.

So, let's make your cake, shall we?

(and PS, we do eat cake on our weight loss plans!)

PURPOSE

We are on earth to do His work for His glory. And that is reflected in our daily living. When we align our desires with His will, He makes the path more visible and much easier to travel. This journal will serve as a daily reminder to keep you on course. The purpose of this journal is to:

1. Help you identify your goals, big or small, with God's help.
2. Attach plans of intention associated with those goals so you know your steps of action and how to pray.
3. Use God as your guide in the goal planning and intentions.
4. Grow closer to God and get comfortable with trusting His leading.
5. Stay accountable and in a positive frame of mind daily to help you reach your goal.

Ready to get started? I know God is!

GOAL SETTING

Write down all of your desires. No matter how big or small, list them here. The only rule is to make sure these are things that you can actually attempt to affect through your daily efforts. This journal is a *goal* journal. So while there is probably an awesome journal out there to write down your prayer requests for your husband's sister's dog to be healed, this is not the place . . . unless you are a veterinarian working to master the revolutionary surgery that said dog needs—you feel me? Further down the line you will need to be able to attach actions to each of these that you can be working towards. Keep that in mind as you work on your list.

We are setting the foundation for your goals and action steps on this page! Write as many as you can think of and don't overthink it. We are just writing ideas right now—nothing is set in stone!

Here are a few of mine for example:

> *Be a more attentive wife.*
> *Put motherhood first.*
> *Have less debt.*
> *Grow my membership to 1,000 members.*
> *Improve physical health.*
> *Improve mental health.*
> *Slow down and cherish the days I am in.*

There is no rhyme or reason to this. They can be as specific as you'd like them to be, but remember, we are moving to action steps next, so we are going to have to be able to break these down further into something that is workable.

WRITE DOWN YOUR DESIRES HERE:
Come back and star your top two to three desires.

GOAL NARROWING

Now here comes the hard part that I know you are going to want to skip. DON'T SKIP IT! For the next week (or longer), pray over this page. Get quiet with God and ask Him to reveal your areas of focus. You have written down your fleshly desires and now it is time to ask God to meet you there and place on your heart whether these are in His will to pursue.

One mistake we tend to make is wanting to tackle them all at once, which sets us up for overload and then eventually avoidance of any goals at all. DO NOT DO THAT. Ask God to reveal your top two or three goals of focus. If He reveals something that is not on your list, add it. If He tells you something is a "hard no," cross it off.

Come back to this page and pray and pray again until you feel consistently comfortable with the same goals. These should feel easy on your heart and your gut. If they don't, keep praying. If they do, only then should you move on.

Example prayer: Lord, I am coming to You today with my goals at Your feet. I have been working for my flesh for far too long, and it has gotten me nowhere. I am surrendering my goals to You and am ready to step into Your desires for me. Reveal to me where You want me to go, Lord, and let me remain focused on You. Show me which path to take and establish my steps. Let Your desires become my desires. Let my efforts and my results bring You glory. Amen.

CREATING INTENTIONS

Okay, so I am trusting that you are on this page because you are feeling comfortable after your prayer time and are locked in to your top two or three goals from the previous page. If you just got a knot in your stomach because you aren't sure, go back and pray some more and come back when you are ready!

In this section, we are focusing on breaking down those goals into simple daily action steps that can be done to get us there—we are calling them intentions. While we will definitely pray over these goals regularly, we also want to make sure we are putting in the practical work that is needed. After all, God can't do His part if we aren't willing to at least show up.

For the sake of this journal, a daily intention is simply a step we can take for today that will help us get closer to the goal. I like to develop these steps by visualizing the end. For instance, imagine that you have reached your goal, what did you do to get there? What are some behaviors that you think you could adopt to make this goal a reality?

On the next page, I want you to list three to five intentions that you think would be beneficial for reaching your goal. Let them be a variety of things so that you know you will be able to accomplish at least one consistently.

I am pausing here to remind you that these intentions should not feel miserable or near impossible to execute. They should take into account your schedule and responsibilities and should be realistic for your daily life and habits.

Let's use Suzy as an example:

Suzy is a mom of three and at least one of her kids has a sports practice nearly every evening of the week. Her husband works late, leaving her with sports and dinner duties. She works full time at a desk job and often has delicious lunches catered in by her boss. Because she gets lunch at work, she tries to work through her lunch so she can get off at noon on Fridays.

Suzy gets off work at 5 p.m. just to speed around trying to get all the kids and their equipment where they need to go. She usually hits the drive-thru with the kids on the way home. They eat in the car and then rush around trying to get baths and homework done so they can get to bed. Suzy does not fall asleep until 11:00 p.m. most nights because she tries to stay awake and have some alone time, plus spend a little time with her husband. Even though usually still exhausted, Suzy wakes up at 5:30 a.m. to get breakfast ready for her family. She gets her kids on the bus and then herself ready for work so she can leave by 7:15 a.m.

Suzy's goal is to lose ten pounds.

The intentions she chose for this goal were:
- Walk five miles today (even though she can't find time to exercise at all currently).
- Only drink water today (even though she drinks four diet colas every day to keep her energized).
- Only eat 1,200 calories today (even though she hasn't gone under 2,000 calories for three weeks straight).

With such intense intentions, you may have guessed that Suzy wouldn't stick to her plan for very long, but the honest truth is, like Suzy, we set ourselves up for extreme behavior changes all the time. They sound so noble and make her feel so motivated in the moment, but these intense intentions will also be the exact reason that Suzy eventually begins to let this goal journal collect dust, avoiding her goals yet again. She set her bar too high and with each passing day her goal will seem less exciting now that she outlined such hard-to-reach obstacles for herself.

Make sure your intentions are things that challenge you to be better, but don't feel impossible to implement after one day. We want them to feel more like "just a little extra effort today" rather than "killing yourself in the name of your goal" today. Oftentimes, we don't reach our goal because we outlined action steps that were too impossible to stick to consistently. So find something that you can stick to. And once you stick to it for awhile, and it becomes routine, you can always add more or change it up.

So here are some better intentions for Suzy to help her lose that ten pounds:

- Walk for ten minutes today during my break.
- Make sure to get my ounces of water in today, still enjoying my diet cola.
- Track my intake today, regardless if I go over my calories, just so I can begin to get a better idea of how my nutrition is affecting my weight loss attempts.

These are just baby versions of the previous actions but are much more attainable when starting out! There is always room for Suzy to increase her action steps later on, but Suzy's main focus for now is to STICK to the ones she has!

From here write the three goals you chose on the top line of the next pages. Then, list doable actions that you could attempt to help you reach that goal. Keep in mind that the repetition of these actions are what is going to get you closer to meeting that goal, so on these pages, more is not always better. Spend some time focusing in on things you know you could do.

GOAL:

Intention: _____
Intention: _____
Intention: _____
Intention: _____
Intention: _____

GOAL:

Intention: _____
Intention: _____
Intention: _____
Intention: _____
Intention: _____

GOAL:

Intention: _____
Intention: _____
Intention: _____
Intention: _____
Intention: _____

GOAL:

Intention: _____
Intention: _____
Intention: _____
Intention: _____
Intention: _____

LET'S GET STARTED!

Yay! You have made it!! I am so proud of you for being realistic and clear with your goals and action steps. And now for the fun part—making those goals a REALITY!

For the next sixty days, you will work towards these goals through repetition, prayer, biblical encouragement, and gratitude. This is a well-rounded approach for:

- Remembering and actively claiming what you already have to be thankful for.
- Meditating on encouraging Bible verses to support a goal-reaching mindset.
- Reminding yourself of your goals and choosing an intention to focus on each day.
- Spending quiet, uninterrupted time with God.
- Communicating with the Lord about the goals and intentions that you have set out to reach.
- Following up on your previous day's effort to keep yourself accountable.

HOW IT WORKS:

Gratitude: Each day you will start with a gratitude statement. It does not have to be related to your goals and intentions, or it can be! It is totally up to you and what you are feeling thankful for each day. Begin the day thanking God for your blessings as a positive reminder that while you are headed into the day ready to put forth effort for growth, you won't allow yourself to forget how much God has already done for you. I like to think that this habit starts us above neutral every day, already praising Him for what we have instead of telling Him more of what we need.

Reflect: Before beginning your next day, go back to the page before and summarize how your goal/intention went from the previous entry. Don't skip this part. Using this step can be very powerful in ensuring you work on your intention each day and in turn see the progress you desire.

Goals/Intentions: You will then list your three goals. Write them out each and every day. Just seeing the goals in print will remind you of your focus. From there, pick ONE goal to focus on that day and choose an action step from your intention list. Write it down.

Rewrite: Look up the Bible verse for the day and rewrite it. Read the verses before and after to get a context of what you are writing.

Be Still: One minute of quiet time. Spend time here reflecting on the Bible verse, your goals, your intention, and God's goodness.

Pray: Write your prayer. This doesn't have to be scripted or perfect. You can declare thankfulness or ask for help. It can be a paragraph or three words long. The focus here is staying in true conversation with God to feel that closeness with Him as you prepare for your day.

Day _____   Date _____

Gratitude:
I am grateful for: _mine and my family's health_ _____
_____

Reflect:
How did your previous day's intention go? Write here.
Yesterday's intention was to make it to my pilates class. I had to work late so I didn't make it, but I did do 10 minutes of stretching before bed.

Goals:
Goal: _Put motherhood first._

Goal: _Have less debt._

Goal: _Improve physical health._

Pray over the goals written above. Which one stands out most today? Circle or highlight today's goal focus and write one intention related to that goal below.

Intention:
Go for a 2 mile walk outside.
_____
_____
_____
_____

2 Corinthians 12:9
[Look up verse and write it below.]

Rewrite:
"My grace is sufficient for you, for my power is made perfect in weakness." Therefore I will boast all the more gladly of my weaknesses, so that the power of Christ may rest upon me.

Be Still:
Sit still. Talk to God. Tell Him your worries and your hopes. Listen for Him.

Pray:
Write your specific prayer here. Write the words on your heart.

Lord, I am weak. You have gotten me to where I am in this life and You will guide me to my next place how You see fit. Let me remember this when I try to control my walk and my days. Show me Your way, Lord, and let me listen so that You can shine through me. Let others see You through me.

Day _____   Date _____

Gratitude:
I am grateful for: _____
_____
_____

Reflect:
How did your previous day's intention go? Write here.
_____
_____
_____

Goals:
Goal: _____

Goal: _____

Goal: _____

Pray over the goals written above. Which one stands out most today? Circle or highlight today's goal focus and write one intention related to that goal below.

Intention:
_____
_____
_____
_____

Acts 20:24
[Look up verse and write it below.]

Rewrite:

_____
_____
_____
_____

Be Still:
Sit still. Talk to God. Tell Him your worries and your hopes. Listen for Him.

Pray:
Write your specific prayer here. Write the words on your heart.

Day _____   Date _____

Gratitude:
I am grateful for: _____
_____
_____

Reflect:
How did your previous day's intention go? Write here.
_____
_____
_____

Goals:
Goal: _____

Goal: _____

Goal: _____

Pray over the goals written above. Which one stands out most today? Circle or highlight today's goal focus and write one intention related to that goal below.

Intention:
_____
_____
_____
_____
_____

Ephesians 2:8-10
[Look up verse and write it below.]

Rewrite:

Be Still:
Sit still. Talk to God. Tell Him your worries and your hopes. Listen for Him.

Pray:
Write your specific prayer here. Write the words on your heart.

Day _____   Date _____

Gratitude:
I am grateful for: _____

_____

_____

Reflect:
How did your previous day's intention go? Write here.

_____

_____

_____

Goals:
Goal: _____

Goal: _____

Goal: _____

Pray over the goals written above. Which one stands out most today? Circle or highlight today's goal focus and write one intention related to that goal below.

Intention:

_____

_____

_____

_____

James 1: 22-25
[Look up verse and write it below.]

Rewrite:
_____
_____
_____
_____

Be Still:
Sit still. Talk to God. Tell Him your worries and your hopes. Listen for Him.

Pray:
Write your specific prayer here. Write the words on your heart.

Day _____ Date _____

Gratitude:
I am grateful for: _____
_____
_____

Reflect:
How did your previous day's intention go? Write here.
_____
_____

Goals:
Goal: _____

Goal: _____

Goal: _____

Pray over the goals written above. Which one stands out most today? Circle or highlight today's goal focus and write one intention related to that goal below.

Intention:
_____
_____
_____
_____
_____

Habakkuk 2:3
[Look up verse and write it below.]

Rewrite:

Be Still:
Sit still. Talk to God. Tell Him your worries and your hopes. Listen for Him.

Pray:
Write your specific prayer here. Write the words on your heart.

Day _____ *Date* _____

Gratitude:
I am grateful for: _____
_____
_____

Reflect:
How did your previous day's intention go? Write here.
_____
_____
_____

Goals:
Goal: _____

Goal: _____

Goal: _____

Pray over the goals written above. Which one stands out most today? Circle or highlight today's goal focus and write one intention related to that goal below.

Intention:
_____
_____
_____
_____
_____

2 Corinthians 12:9
[Look up verse and write it below.]

Rewrite:

Be Still:
Sit still. Talk to God. Tell Him your worries and your hopes. Listen for Him.

Pray:
Write your specific prayer here. Write the words on your heart.

Day _____ Date _____

Gratitude:
I am grateful for: _____
_____
_____

Reflect:
How did your previous day's intention go? Write here.
_____
_____
_____

Goals:
Goal: _____

Goal: _____

Goal: _____

Pray over the goals written above. Which one stands out most today? Circle or highlight today's goal focus and write one intention related to that goal below.

Intention:
_____
_____
_____
_____

1 Peter 4:10
[Look up verse and write it below.]

Rewrite:

Be Still:
Sit still. Talk to God. Tell Him your worries and your hopes. Listen for Him.

Pray:
Write your specific prayer here. Write the words on your heart.

Day _____ *Date* _____

Gratitude:
I am grateful for: _____
_____
_____

Reflect:
How did your previous day's intention go? Write here.
_____
_____
_____

Goals:
Goal: _____

Goal: _____

Goal: _____

Pray over the goals written above. Which one stands out most today? Circle or highlight today's goal focus and write one intention related to that goal below.

Intention:
_____
_____
_____
_____
_____

Romans 15:13
[Look up verse and write it below.]

Rewrite:

_____
_____
_____
_____

Be Still:
Sit still. Talk to God. Tell Him your worries and your hopes. Listen for Him.

Pray:
Write your specific prayer here. Write the words on your heart.

Day _____ *Date* _____

Gratitude:
I am grateful for: _____
_____
_____

Reflect:
How did your previous day's intention go? Write here.
_____
_____
_____

Goals:
Goal: _____

Goal: _____

Goal: _____

Pray over the goals written above. Which one stands out most today? Circle or highlight today's goal focus and write one intention related to that goal below.

Intention:
_____
_____
_____
_____
_____

1 Peter 5:6-7
[Look up verse and write it below.]

Rewrite:

Be Still:
Sit still. Talk to God. Tell Him your worries and your hopes. Listen for Him.

Pray:
Write your specific prayer here. Write the words on your heart.

Day _____   *Date* _____

Gratitude:
I am grateful for: _____
_____
_____

Reflect:
How did your previous day's intention go? Write here.
_____
_____
_____

Goals:
Goal: _____

Goal: _____

Goal: _____

Pray over the goals written above. Which one stands out most today? Circle or highlight today's goal focus and write one intention related to that goal below.

Intention:
_____
_____
_____
_____
_____

Psalm 127:1

[Look up verse and write it below.]

Rewrite:

_____
_____
_____
_____

Be Still:

Sit still. Talk to God. Tell Him your worries and your hopes. Listen for Him.

Pray:

Write your specific prayer here. Write the words on your heart.

Day _____ *Date* _____

Gratitude:
I am grateful for: _____
_____
_____

Reflect:
How did your previous day's intention go? Write here.
_____
_____
_____

Goals:
Goal: _____

Goal: _____

Goal: _____

Pray over the goals written above. Which one stands out most today? Circle or highlight today's goal focus and write one intention related to that goal below.

Intention:
_____
_____
_____
_____
_____

Romans 12:2
[Look up verse and write it below.]

Rewrite:

Be Still:
Sit still. Talk to God. Tell Him your worries and your hopes. Listen for Him.

Pray:
Write your specific prayer here. Write the words on your heart.

Day _____   Date _____

Gratitude:
I am grateful for: _____
_____
_____

Reflect:
How did your previous day's intention go? Write here.
_____
_____
_____

Goals:
Goal: _____

Goal: _____

Goal: _____

Pray over the goals written above. Which one stands out most today? Circle or highlight today's goal focus and write one intention related to that goal below.

Intention:
_____
_____
_____
_____
_____

Ephesians 6:24
[Look up verse and write it below.]

Rewrite:

_____

_____

_____

_____

Be Still:
Sit still. Talk to God. Tell Him your worries and your hopes. Listen for Him.

Pray:
Write your specific prayer here. Write the words on your heart.

_____

_____

_____

_____

_____

_____

_____

_____

_____

Day _____   Date _____

Gratitude:
I am grateful for: _____
_____
_____

Reflect:
How did your previous day's intention go? Write here.
_____
_____
_____

Goals:
Goal: _____

Goal: _____

Goal: _____

Pray over the goals written above. Which one stands out most today? Circle or highlight today's goal focus and write one intention related to that goal below.

Intention:
_____
_____
_____
_____

Deuteronomy 2:3
[Look up verse and write it below.]

Rewrite:

Be Still:
Sit still. Talk to God. Tell Him your worries and your hopes. Listen for Him.

Pray:
Write your specific prayer here. Write the words on your heart.

Day _____ Date _____

Gratitude:
I am grateful for: _____
_____
_____

Reflect:
How did your previous day's intention go? Write here.
_____
_____
_____

Goals:
Goal: _____

Goal: _____

Goal: _____

Pray over the goals written above. Which one stands out most today? Circle or highlight today's goal focus and write one intention related to that goal below.

Intention:
_____
_____
_____
_____
_____
_____

Ezra 10:4

[Look up verse and write it below.]

Rewrite:

Be Still:
Sit still. Talk to God. Tell Him your worries and your hopes. Listen for Him.

Pray:
Write your specific prayer here. Write the words on your heart.

Day _____ *Date* _____

Gratitude:
I am grateful for: _____
_____
_____

Reflect:
How did your previous day's intention go? Write here.
_____
_____
_____

Goals:
Goal: _____

Goal: _____

Goal: _____

Pray over the goals written above. Which one stands out most today? Circle or highlight today's goal focus and write one intention related to that goal below.

Intention:
_____
_____
_____
_____
_____

John 4:34

[Look up verse and write it below.]

Rewrite:

_____

_____

_____

_____

Be Still:
Sit still. Talk to God. Tell Him your worries and your hopes. Listen for Him.

Pray:
Write your specific prayer here. Write the words on your heart.

Day _____ *Date* _____

Gratitude:
I am grateful for: _____
_____
_____

Reflect:
How did your previous day's intention go? Write here.
_____
_____
_____

Goals:
Goal: _____

Goal: _____

Goal: _____

Pray over the goals written above. Which one stands out most today? Circle or highlight today's goal focus and write one intention related to that goal below.

Intention:
_____
_____
_____
_____
_____

Romans 8:5-6
[Look up verse and write it below.]

Rewrite:

Be Still:
Sit still. Talk to God. Tell Him your worries and your hopes. Listen for Him.

Pray:
Write your specific prayer here. Write the words on your heart.

Day _____ Date _____

Gratitude:
I am grateful for: _____
_____
_____

Reflect:
How did your previous day's intention go? Write here.
_____
_____
_____

Goals:
Goal: _____

Goal: _____

Goal: _____

Pray over the goals written above. Which one stands out most today? Circle or highlight today's goal focus and write one intention related to that goal below.

Intention:
_____
_____
_____
_____

Psalm 73:25-26
[Look up verse and write it below.]

Rewrite:

Be Still:
Sit still. Talk to God. Tell Him your worries and your hopes. Listen for Him.

Pray:
Write your specific prayer here. Write the words on your heart.

Day _____ Date _____

Gratitude:
I am grateful for: _____

_____

_____

Reflect:
How did your previous day's intention go? Write here.

_____

_____

_____

Goals:
Goal: _____

Goal: _____

Goal: _____

Pray over the goals written above. Which one stands out most today? Circle or highlight today's goal focus and write one intention related to that goal below.

Intention:

_____

_____

_____

_____

Psalm 86:11-12
[Look up verse and write it below.]

Rewrite:

_____

_____

_____

_____

Be Still:
Sit still. Talk to God. Tell Him your worries and your hopes. Listen for Him.

Pray:
Write your specific prayer here. Write the words on your heart.

Day _____   Date _____

Gratitude:
I am grateful for: _____
_____
_____

Reflect:
How did your previous day's intention go? Write here.
_____
_____
_____

Goals:

Goal: _____

Goal: _____

Goal: _____

Pray over the goals written above. Which one stands out most today? Circle or highlight today's goal focus and write one intention related to that goal below.

Intention:
_____
_____
_____
_____
_____

2 Corinthians 10:3-5
[Look up verse and write it below.]

Rewrite:

Be Still:
Sit still. Talk to God. Tell Him your worries and your hopes. Listen for Him.

Pray:
Write your specific prayer here. Write the words on your heart.

Day _____ Date _____

Gratitude:
I am grateful for: _____
_____
_____

Reflect:
How did your previous day's intention go? Write here.
_____
_____
_____

Goals:
Goal: _____

Goal: _____

Goal: _____

Pray over the goals written above. Which one stands out most today? Circle or highlight today's goal focus and write one intention related to that goal below.

Intention:
_____
_____
_____
_____
_____

2 Peter 1:5-6
[Look up verse and write it below.]

Rewrite:
_____
_____
_____
_____

Be Still:
Sit still. Talk to God. Tell Him your worries and your hopes. Listen for Him.

Pray:
Write your specific prayer here. Write the words on your heart.

Day

Date

Gratitude:
I am grateful for: _____
_____
_____

Reflect:
How did your previous day's intention go? Write here.
_____
_____
_____

Goals:
Goal: _____

Goal: _____

Goal: _____

Pray over the goals written above. Which one stands out most today? Circle or highlight today's goal focus and write one intention related to that goal below.

Intention:
_____
_____
_____
_____

Isaiah 26:3-4
[Look up verse and write it below.]

Rewrite:
_____
_____
_____
_____

Be Still:
Sit still. Talk to God. Tell Him your worries and your hopes. Listen for Him.

Pray:
Write your specific prayer here. Write the words on your heart.

Day _____   Date _____

Gratitude:
I am grateful for: _____
_____
_____

Reflect:
How did your previous day's intention go? Write here.
_____
_____
_____

Goals:
Goal: _____

Goal: _____

Goal: _____

Pray over the goals written above. Which one stands out most today? Circle or highlight today's goal focus and write one intention related to that goal below.

Intention:
_____
_____
_____
_____
_____

Isaiah 43:2
[Look up verse and write it below.]

Rewrite:

Be Still:
Sit still. Talk to God. Tell Him your worries and your hopes. Listen for Him.

Pray:
Write your specific prayer here. Write the words on your heart.

Day _____ Date _____

Gratitude:
I am grateful for: _____
_____
_____

Reflect:
How did your previous day's intention go? Write here.
_____
_____
_____

Goals:
Goal: _____

Goal: _____

Goal: _____

Pray over the goals written above. Which one stands out most today? Circle or highlight today's goal focus and write one intention related to that goal below.

Intention:
_____
_____
_____
_____
_____

Jeremiah 29:11
[Look up verse and write it below.]

Rewrite:
_____
_____
_____
_____

Be Still:
Sit still. Talk to God. Tell Him your worries and your hopes. Listen for Him.

Pray:
Write your specific prayer here. Write the words on your heart.

Day _____ Date _____

Gratitude:
I am grateful for: _____
_____
_____

Reflect:
How did your previous day's intention go? Write here.
_____
_____
_____

Goals:
Goal: _____

Goal: _____

Goal: _____

Pray over the goals written above. Which one stands out most today? Circle or highlight today's goal focus and write one intention related to that goal below.

Intention:
_____
_____
_____
_____
_____

Ephesians 5:1-2
[Look up verse and write it below.]

Rewrite:

Be Still:
Sit still. Talk to God. Tell Him your worries and your hopes. Listen for Him.

Pray:
Write your specific prayer here. Write the words on your heart.

Day _____ Date _____

Gratitude:
I am grateful for: _____
_____
_____

Reflect:
How did your previous day's intention go? Write here.
_____
_____
_____

Goals:
Goal: _____

Goal: _____

Goal: _____

Pray over the goals written above. Which one stands out most today? Circle or highlight today's goal focus and write one intention related to that goal below.

Intention:
_____
_____
_____
_____
_____

Philippians 4:6
[Look up verse and write it below.]

Rewrite:

_____
_____
_____

Be Still:
Sit still. Talk to God. Tell Him your worries and your hopes. Listen for Him.

Pray:
Write your specific prayer here. Write the words on your heart.

_____
_____
_____
_____
_____
_____
_____
_____
_____
_____
_____
_____

Day _____ *Date* _____

Gratitude:
I am grateful for: _____
_____
_____
_____

Reflect:
How did your previous day's intention go? Write here.
_____
_____
_____

Goals:
Goal: _____

Goal: _____

Goal: _____

Pray over the goals written above. Which one stands out most today? Circle or highlight today's goal focus and write one intention related to that goal below.

Intention:
_____
_____
_____
_____
_____

2 Timothy 1:7
[Look up verse and write it below.]

Rewrite:

Be Still:
Sit still. Talk to God. Tell Him your worries and your hopes. Listen for Him.

Pray:
Write your specific prayer here. Write the words on your heart.

Day _____ Date _____

Gratitude:
I am grateful for: _____
_____
_____

Reflect:
How did your previous day's intention go? Write here.
_____
_____
_____

Goals:
Goal: _____

Goal: _____

Goal: _____

Pray over the goals written above. Which one stands out most today? Circle or highlight today's goal focus and write one intention related to that goal below.

Intention:
_____
_____
_____
_____
_____

Hebrews 12:11
[Look up verse and write it below.]

Rewrite:

Be Still:
Sit still. Talk to God. Tell Him your worries and your hopes. Listen for Him.

Pray:
Write your specific prayer here. Write the words on your heart.

Day _____ Date _____

Gratitude:
I am grateful for: _____
_____
_____

Reflect:
How did your previous day's intention go? Write here.
_____
_____
_____

Goals:
Goal: _____

Goal: _____

Goal: _____

Pray over the goals written above. Which one stands out most today? Circle or highlight today's goal focus and write one intention related to that goal below.

Intention:
_____
_____
_____
_____
_____

Exodus 14:14
[Look up verse and write it below.]

Rewrite:

Be Still:
Sit still. Talk to God. Tell Him your worries and your hopes. Listen for Him.

Pray:
Write your specific prayer here. Write the words on your heart.

Day _____ *Date* _____

Gratitude:
I am grateful for: _____
_____
_____

Reflect:
How did your previous day's intention go? Write here.
_____
_____
_____

Goals:
Goal: _____

Goal: _____

Goal: _____

Pray over the goals written above. Which one stands out most today? Circle or highlight today's goal focus and write one intention related to that goal below.

Intention:
_____
_____
_____
_____
_____

Romans 8:27-28
[Look up verse and write it below.]

Rewrite:

Be Still:
Sit still. Talk to God. Tell Him your worries and your hopes. Listen for Him.

Pray:
Write your specific prayer here. Write the words on your heart.

Day _____ Date _____

Gratitude:
I am grateful for: _____
_____
_____

Reflect:
How did your previous day's intention go? Write here.
_____
_____
_____

Goals:
Goal: _____

Goal: _____

Goal: _____

Pray over the goals written above. Which one stands out most today? Circle or highlight today's goal focus and write one intention related to that goal below.

Intention:
_____
_____
_____
_____
_____

Proverbs 3:5-6
[Look up verse and write it below.]

Rewrite:

Be Still:
Sit still. Talk to God. Tell Him your worries and your hopes. Listen for Him.

Pray:
Write your specific prayer here. Write the words on your heart.

Day _____ Date _____

Gratitude:
I am grateful for: _____
_____
_____

Reflect:
How did your previous day's intention go? Write here.
_____
_____
_____

Goals:
Goal: _____

Goal: _____

Goal: _____

Pray over the goals written above. Which one stands out most today? Circle or highlight today's goal focus and write one intention related to that goal below.

Intention:
_____
_____
_____
_____

John 16:33
[Look up verse and write it below.]

Rewrite:
___
___
___
___

Be Still:
Sit still. Talk to God. Tell Him your worries and your hopes. Listen for Him.

Pray:
Write your specific prayer here. Write the words on your heart.

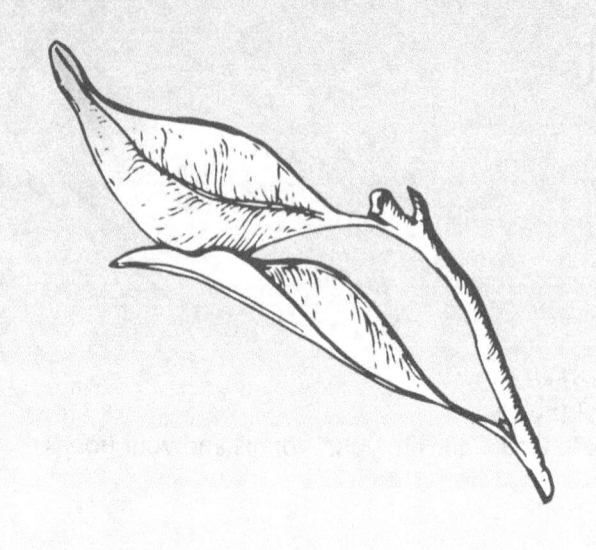

For the one who sows to his own flesh will from the flesh reap corruption, but the one who sows to the Spirit will from the Spirit reap eternal life. And let us not grow weary of doing good, for in due season we will reap, if we do not give up.
Galatians 6:8-9

Do not conform to the pattern of
this world, but be transformed by the
renewing of your mind. Then you will be
able to test and approve what God's will
is—his good, pleasing and perfect will.
Romans 12:2 NIV

Day _____ *Date* _____

Gratitude:
I am grateful for: _____
_____
_____

Reflect:
How did your previous day's intention go? Write here.
_____
_____

Goals:
Goal: _____

Goal: _____

Goal: _____

Pray over the goals written above. Which one stands out most today? Circle or highlight today's goal focus and write one intention related to that goal below.

Intention:
_____
_____
_____
_____

Hebrews 11:1

[Look up verse and write it below.]

Rewrite:

_____
_____
_____

Be Still:
Sit still. Talk to God. Tell Him your worries and your hopes. Listen for Him.

Pray:
Write your specific prayer here. Write the words on your heart.

_____
_____
_____
_____
_____
_____
_____
_____
_____
_____

Day _____   Date _____

Gratitude:
I am grateful for: _____
_____
_____

Reflect:
How did your previous day's intention go? Write here.
_____
_____

Goals:
Goal: _____

Goal: _____

Goal: _____

Pray over the goals written above. Which one stands out most today? Circle or highlight today's goal focus and write one intention related to that goal below.

Intention:
_____
_____
_____
_____

Isaiah 54:10
[Look up verse and write it below.]

Rewrite:

Be Still:
Sit still. Talk to God. Tell Him your worries and your hopes. Listen for Him.

Pray:
Write your specific prayer here. Write the words on your heart.

Day _____ *Date* _____

Gratitude:
I am grateful for: _____
_____
_____

Reflect:
How did your previous day's intention go? Write here.
_____
_____
_____

Goals:
Goal: _____

Goal: _____

Goal: _____

Pray over the goals written above. Which one stands out most today? Circle or highlight today's goal focus and write one intention related to that goal below.

Intention:
_____
_____
_____
_____
_____

Matthew 6:33

[Look up verse and write it below.]

Rewrite:

_____
_____
_____
_____

Be Still:
Sit still. Talk to God. Tell Him your worries and your hopes. Listen for Him.

Pray:
Write your specific prayer here. Write the words on your heart.

Day _____   Date _____

Gratitude:
I am grateful for: _____
_____
_____

Reflect:
How did your previous day's intention go? Write here.
_____
_____
_____

Goals:

Goal: _____

Goal: _____

Goal: _____

Pray over the goals written above. Which one stands out most today? Circle or highlight today's goal focus and write one intention related to that goal below.

Intention:
_____
_____
_____
_____

Psalm 107:9
[Look up verse and write it below.]

Rewrite:

Be Still:
Sit still. Talk to God. Tell Him your worries and your hopes. Listen for Him.

Pray:
Write your specific prayer here. Write the words on your heart.

Day _____ *Date* _____

Gratitude:
I am grateful for: _____
_____
_____

Reflect:
How did your previous day's intention go? Write here.
_____
_____
_____

Goals:
Goal: _____

Goal: _____

Goal: _____

Pray over the goals written above. Which one stands out most today? Circle or highlight today's goal focus and write one intention related to that goal below.

Intention:
_____
_____
_____
_____
_____

Psalm 85:12-13
[Look up verse and write it below.]

Rewrite:

Be Still:
Sit still. Talk to God. Tell Him your worries and your hopes. Listen for Him.

Pray:
Write your specific prayer here. Write the words on your heart.

Day _____   Date _____

Gratitude:
I am grateful for: _____
_____
_____

Reflect:
How did your previous day's intention go? Write here.
_____
_____
_____

Goals:
Goal: _____

Goal: _____

Goal: _____

Pray over the goals written above. Which one stands out most today? Circle or highlight today's goal focus and write one intention related to that goal below.

Intention:
_____
_____
_____
_____

Romans 5:19
[Look up verse and write it below.]

Rewrite:

_____

_____

_____

_____

Be Still:
Sit still. Talk to God. Tell Him your worries and your hopes. Listen for Him.

Pray:
Write your specific prayer here. Write the words on your heart.

Day _____   Date _____

Gratitude:
I am grateful for: _____
_____
_____

Reflect:
How did your previous day's intention go? Write here.
_____
_____
_____

Goals:
Goal: _____

Goal: _____

Goal: _____

Pray over the goals written above. Which one stands out most today? Circle or highlight today's goal focus and write one intention related to that goal below.

Intention:
_____
_____
_____
_____
_____

Proverbs 15:32-33

[Look up verse and write it below.]

Rewrite:

_____
_____
_____
_____

Be Still:
Sit still. Talk to God. Tell Him your worries and your hopes. Listen for Him.

Pray:
Write your specific prayer here. Write the words on your heart.

Day _____   Date _____

Gratitude:
I am grateful for: _____
_____
_____

Reflect:
How did your previous day's intention go? Write here.
_____
_____
_____

Goals:
Goal: _____

Goal: _____

Goal: _____

Pray over the goals written above. Which one stands out most today? Circle or highlight today's goal focus and write one intention related to that goal below.

Intention:

_____
_____
_____
_____

Micah 7:7
[Look up verse and write it below.]

Rewrite:

_____
_____
_____
_____

Be Still:
Sit still. Talk to God. Tell Him your worries and your hopes. Listen for Him.

Pray:
Write your specific prayer here. Write the words on your heart.

Day _____ Date _____

Gratitude:
I am grateful for: _____
_____
_____

Reflect:
How did your previous day's intention go? Write here.
_____
_____
_____

Goals:
Goal: _____

Goal: _____

Goal: _____

Pray over the goals written above. Which one stands out most today? Circle or highlight today's goal focus and write one intention related to that goal below.

Intention:
_____
_____
_____
_____
_____

Romans 5:3-5
[Look up verse and write it below.]

Rewrite:

_____
_____
_____

Be Still:
Sit still. Talk to God. Tell Him your worries and your hopes. Listen for Him.

Pray:
Write your specific prayer here. Write the words on your heart.

_____
_____
_____
_____
_____
_____
_____
_____
_____

Day _____   Date _____

Gratitude:
I am grateful for: _____
_____
_____
_____

Reflect:
How did your previous day's intention go? Write here.
_____
_____
_____

Goals:
Goal: _____

Goal: _____

Goal: _____

Pray over the goals written above. Which one stands out most today? Circle or highlight today's goal focus and write one intention related to that goal below.

Intention:
_____
_____
_____
_____

Psalm 16:8

[Look up verse and write it below.]

Rewrite:

_____

_____

_____

_____

Be Still:
Sit still. Talk to God. Tell Him your worries and your hopes. Listen for Him.

Pray:
Write your specific prayer here. Write the words on your heart.

Day _____   Date _____

Gratitude:
I am grateful for: _____
_____
_____

Reflect:
How did your previous day's intention go? Write here.
_____
_____
_____

Goals:
Goal: _____

Goal: _____

Goal: _____

Pray over the goals written above. Which one stands out most today? Circle or highlight today's goal focus and write one intention related to that goal below.

Intention:
_____
_____
_____
_____

Lamentations 3:22-24
[Look up verse and write it below.]

Rewrite:

_____

_____

_____

_____

Be Still:
Sit still. Talk to God. Tell Him your worries and your hopes. Listen for Him.

Pray:
Write your specific prayer here. Write the words on your heart.

Day _____ *Date* _____

Gratitude:
I am grateful for: _____
_____
_____

Reflect:
How did your previous day's intention go? Write here.
_____
_____
_____

Goals:
Goal: _____

Goal: _____

Goal: _____

Pray over the goals written above. Which one stands out most today? Circle or highlight today's goal focus and write one intention related to that goal below.

Intention:
_____
_____
_____
_____
_____

John 14:27

[Look up verse and write it below.]

Rewrite:

Be Still:
Sit still. Talk to God. Tell Him your worries and your hopes. Listen for Him.

Pray:
Write your specific prayer here. Write the words on your heart.

Day _____ *Date* _____

Gratitude:
I am grateful for: _____
_____
_____

Reflect:
How did your previous day's intention go? Write here.
_____
_____
_____

Goals:
Goal: _____

Goal: _____

Goal: _____

Pray over the goals written above. Which one stands out most today? Circle or highlight today's goal focus and write one intention related to that goal below.

Intention:
_____
_____
_____
_____
_____

Malachi 4:2
[Look up verse and write it below.]

Rewrite:

Be Still:
Sit still. Talk to God. Tell Him your worries and your hopes. Listen for Him.

Pray:
Write your specific prayer here. Write the words on your heart.

Day _____   Date _____

Gratitude:
I am grateful for: _____
_____
_____

Reflect:
How did your previous day's intention go? Write here.
_____
_____
_____

Goals:
Goal: _____

Goal: _____

Goal: _____

Pray over the goals written above. Which one stands out most today? Circle or highlight today's goal focus and write one intention related to that goal below.

Intention:
_____
_____
_____
_____
_____

James 4:5-7
[Look up verse and write it below.]

Rewrite:
_____
_____
_____
_____

Be Still:
Sit still. Talk to God. Tell Him your worries and your hopes. Listen for Him.

Pray:
Write your specific prayer here. Write the words on your heart.

_____
_____
_____
_____
_____
_____
_____
_____
_____
_____
_____

Day _____   Date _____

Gratitude:
I am grateful for: _____
_____
_____

Reflect:
How did your previous day's intention go? Write here.
_____
_____
_____

Goals:
Goal: _____

Goal: _____

Goal: _____

Pray over the goals written above. Which one stands out most today? Circle or highlight today's goal focus and write one intention related to that goal below.

Intention:
_____
_____
_____
_____
_____

Matthew 4:4
[Look up verse and write it below.]

Rewrite:

_____

_____

_____

Be Still:
Sit still. Talk to God. Tell Him your worries and your hopes. Listen for Him.

Pray:
Write your specific prayer here. Write the words on your heart.

Day _____ *Date* _____

Gratitude:
I am grateful for: _____
_____
_____

Reflect:
How did your previous day's intention go? Write here.
_____
_____
_____

Goals:
Goal: _____

Goal: _____

Goal: _____

Pray over the goals written above. Which one stands out most today? Circle or highlight today's goal focus and write one intention related to that goal below.

Intention:
_____
_____
_____
_____

Psalm 37:3-5
[Look up verse and write it below.]

Rewrite:

Be Still:
Sit still. Talk to God. Tell Him your worries and your hopes. Listen for Him.

Pray:
Write your specific prayer here. Write the words on your heart.

Day _____   Date _____

Gratitude:
I am grateful for: _____
_____
_____

Reflect:
How did your previous day's intention go? Write here.
_____
_____
_____

Goals:
Goal: _____

Goal: _____

Goal: _____

Pray over the goals written above. Which one stands out most today? Circle or highlight today's goal focus and write one intention related to that goal below.

Intention:
_____
_____
_____
_____

Galatians 2:16
[Look up verse and write it below.]

Rewrite:

Be Still:
Sit still. Talk to God. Tell Him your worries and your hopes. Listen for Him.

Pray:
Write your specific prayer here. Write the words on your heart.

Day _____   Date _____

Gratitude:
I am grateful for: _____
_____
_____

Reflect:
How did your previous day's intention go? Write here.
_____
_____
_____

Goals:
Goal: _____

Goal: _____

Goal: _____

Pray over the goals written above. Which one stands out most today? Circle or highlight today's goal focus and write one intention related to that goal below.

Intention:
_____
_____
_____
_____
_____

Ephesians 4:1-2
[Look up verse and write it below.]

Rewrite:

_____
_____
_____
_____

Be Still:
Sit still. Talk to God. Tell Him your worries and your hopes. Listen for Him.

Pray:
Write your specific prayer here. Write the words on your heart.

Day _____   Date _____

Gratitude:
I am grateful for: _____
_____
_____

Reflect:
How did your previous day's intention go? Write here.
_____
_____
_____

Goals:
Goal: _____

Goal: _____

Goal: _____

Pray over the goals written above. Which one stands out most today? Circle or highlight today's goal focus and write one intention related to that goal below.

Intention:
_____
_____
_____
_____
_____

Leviticus 26:3-4
[Look up verse and write it below.]

Rewrite:

Be Still:
Sit still. Talk to God. Tell Him your worries and your hopes. Listen for Him.

Pray:
Write your specific prayer here. Write the words on your heart.

Day _____   Date _____

Gratitude:
I am grateful for: _____
_____
_____

Reflect:
How did your previous day's intention go? Write here.
_____
_____
_____

Goals:
Goal: _____

Goal: _____

Goal: _____

Pray over the goals written above. Which one stands out most today? Circle or highlight today's goal focus and write one intention related to that goal below.

Intention:
_____
_____
_____
_____
_____

Psalm 111:10
[Look up verse and write it below.]

Rewrite:

Be Still:
Sit still. Talk to God. Tell Him your worries and your hopes. Listen for Him.

Pray:
Write your specific prayer here. Write the words on your heart.

Day _____ Date _____

Gratitude:
I am grateful for: _____
_____
_____

Reflect:
How did your previous day's intention go? Write here.
_____
_____
_____

Goals:
Goal: _____

Goal: _____

Goal: _____

Pray over the goals written above. Which one stands out most today? Circle or highlight today's goal focus and write one intention related to that goal below.

Intention:
_____
_____
_____
_____
_____

Luke 9:23-25

[Look up verse and write it below.]

Rewrite:

Be Still:
Sit still. Talk to God. Tell Him your worries and your hopes. Listen for Him.

Pray:
Write your specific prayer here. Write the words on your heart.

Day _____   Date _____

Gratitude:
I am grateful for: _____

_____

_____

Reflect:
How did your previous day's intention go? Write here.

_____

_____

_____

Goals:
Goal: _____

Goal: _____

Goal: _____

Pray over the goals written above. Which one stands out most today? Circle or highlight today's goal focus and write one intention related to that goal below.

Intention:

_____

_____

_____

_____

_____

1 John 5:14-15
[Look up verse and write it below.]

Rewrite:

Be Still:
Sit still. Talk to God. Tell Him your worries and your hopes. Listen for Him.

Pray:
Write your specific prayer here. Write the words on your heart.

Day _____ *Date* _____

Gratitude:
I am grateful for: _____
_____
_____

Reflect:
How did your previous day's intention go? Write here.
_____
_____
_____

Goals:
Goal: _____

Goal: _____

Goal: _____

Pray over the goals written above. Which one stands out most today? Circle or highlight today's goal focus and write one intention related to that goal below.

Intention:
_____
_____
_____
_____
_____

2 Chronicles 7:14
[Look up verse and write it below.]

Rewrite:

Be Still:
Sit still. Talk to God. Tell Him your worries and your hopes. Listen for Him.

Pray:
Write your specific prayer here. Write the words on your heart.

Day _____ Date _____

Gratitude:
I am grateful for: _____
_____
_____

Reflect:
How did your previous day's intention go? Write here.
_____
_____
_____

Goals:
Goal: _____

Goal: _____

Goal: _____

Pray over the goals written above. Which one stands out most today? Circle or highlight today's goal focus and write one intention related to that goal below.

Intention:
_____
_____
_____
_____

Philippians 1:20
[Look up verse and write it below.]

Rewrite:

_____
_____
_____
_____

Be Still:
Sit still. Talk to God. Tell Him your worries and your hopes. Listen for Him.

Pray:
Write your specific prayer here. Write the words on your heart.

Day _____   Date _____

Gratitude:
I am grateful for: _____
_____
_____

Reflect:
How did your previous day's intention go? Write here.
_____
_____
_____

Goals:
Goal: _____

Goal: _____

Goal: _____

Pray over the goals written above. Which one stands out most today? Circle or highlight today's goal focus and write one intention related to that goal below.

Intention:
_____
_____
_____
_____
_____

James 2:17
[Look up verse and write it below.]

Rewrite:

Be Still:
Sit still. Talk to God. Tell Him your worries and your hopes. Listen for Him.

Pray:
Write your specific prayer here. Write the words on your heart.

Day _____ Date _____

Gratitude:
I am grateful for: _____
_____
_____

Reflect:
How did your previous day's intention go? Write here.
_____
_____
_____

Goals:
Goal: _____

Goal: _____

Goal: _____

Pray over the goals written above. Which one stands out most today? Circle or highlight today's goal focus and write one intention related to that goal below.

Intention:
_____
_____
_____
_____
_____

Proverbs 19:21
[Look up verse and write it below.]

Rewrite:

Be Still:
Sit still. Talk to God. Tell Him your worries and your hopes. Listen for Him.

Pray:
Write your specific prayer here. Write the words on your heart.

Day _____   Date _____

Gratitude:
I am grateful for: _____
_____
_____

Reflect:
How did your previous day's intention go? Write here.
_____
_____
_____

Goals:
Goal: _____

Goal: _____

Goal: _____

Pray over the goals written above. Which one stands out most today? Circle or highlight today's goal focus and write one intention related to that goal below.

Intention:
_____
_____
_____
_____
_____

2 Corinthians 9:8
[Look up verse and write it below.]

Rewrite:

Be Still:
Sit still. Talk to God. Tell Him your worries and your hopes. Listen for Him.

Pray:
Write your specific prayer here. Write the words on your heart.

Day _____   Date _____

Gratitude:
I am grateful for: _____
_____
_____

Reflect:
How did your previous day's intention go? Write here.
_____
_____

Goals:
Goal: _____

Goal: _____

Goal: _____

Pray over the goals written above. Which one stands out most today? Circle or highlight today's goal focus and write one intention related to that goal below.

Intention:
_____
_____
_____
_____
_____

Proverbs 16:3
[Look up verse and write it below.]

Rewrite:
_____
_____
_____
_____

Be Still:
Sit still. Talk to God. Tell Him your worries and your hopes. Listen for Him.

Pray:
Write your specific prayer here. Write the words on your heart.

Day _____ Date _____

Gratitude:
I am grateful for: _____
_____
_____

Reflect:
How did your previous day's intention go? Write here.
_____
_____

Goals:
Goal: _____

Goal: _____

Goal: _____

Pray over the goals written above. Which one stands out most today? Circle or highlight today's goal focus and write one intention related to that goal below.

Intention:
_____
_____
_____
_____

Jeremiah 29:11-13
[Look up verse and write it below.]

Rewrite:

_____

_____

_____

_____

Be Still:
Sit still. Talk to God. Tell Him your worries and your hopes. Listen for Him.

Pray:
Write your specific prayer here. Write the words on your heart.

Day _____ Date _____

Gratitude:
I am grateful for: _____
_____
_____

Reflect:
How did your previous day's intention go? Write here.
_____
_____

Goals:
Goal: _____

Goal: _____

Goal: _____

Pray over the goals written above. Which one stands out most today? Circle or highlight today's goal focus and write one intention related to that goal below.

Intention:
_____
_____
_____
_____
_____

James 3:17-18
[Look up verse and write it below.]

Rewrite:

Be Still:
Sit still. Talk to God. Tell Him your worries and your hopes. Listen for Him.

Pray:
Write your specific prayer here. Write the words on your heart.

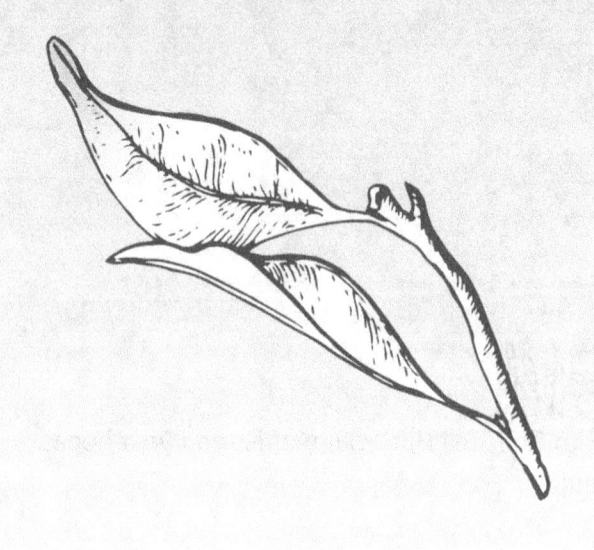

Or do you not know that your body is a temple of the Holy Spirit within you, whom you have from God? You are not your own, for you were bought with a price. So glorify God in your body.
1 Corinthians 6:19-20

And my God will supply every need of yours according to his riches in glory in Christ Jesus.

Philippians 4:19

Reflection Page

Now that you have finished sixty days of carefully planned and intentional goal setting, take a few minutes and write about what you have accomplished.

Note from Constance

Sweet sister, if you have reached this page then that means you have completed sixty days of this goal journal! My prayer is that you are closer to reaching your goals, but even more so that you feel a greater connection to our amazing God. While goals and intentions are important for fulfilling our purpose on this earth, He desires nothing more than that closeness with you.

As we wrap up our time together, I pray that as you move forward in your plans you will first look to the Lord for help and lean on him every day. I have learned the hard way that when I try to achieve something on my own that is not aligned with the Lord's plan, it ends up in heartache and a whole bunch of unnecessary stress! If there is one piece of advice I could offer you, it's to seek Him first in all things, big or small. And then find comfort and confidence in that still small voice that tells you where to go. Using his guidance and direction, paired with your faithfulness, I have no doubt that the result will be fruitful.

Perfect Fit Nutrition is an online weight loss program that not only teaches a realistic and healthy way to lose weight but also helps our clients undo previous fad diet damage.

At Perfect Fit, we teach women how to eat for weight loss without food exclusions while encouraging grace and self-love practices, creating a healthier individual—mind, body and soul.

So many women have grown to believe that weight loss should equal misery or a ton of extra effort that feels outside their norm. However, most women are already stretched thin and can't add much more to their to-do list for a long period of time. This results in constant yo-yo-ing, defeat, and daily food and mental battles!

At Perfect Fit, the focus is on setting practical goals to set you up for success now, but that will evolve into habits that will be manageable in your life forever. It may not always look like all the "experts" say it should, but our clients have weight loss plans that work for their personal lives. This not only makes the process more enjoyable, but it feels less daunting, resulting in them being able to stick to their plans and reach their weight loss goals!

To learn more about losing weight in a way that fits your personal preferences and lifestyle, go to www.perfectfitnutrition.com or email us at **support@perfectfitnutrition.com** for next steps.

www.ingramcontent.com/pod-product-compliance
Lightning Source LLC
LaVergne TN
LVHW022039291224
800080LV00005B/9